Sulcata Tortoise

Complete Owner's Guide

Essential Facts You Have to Know About Buying,
Caring for, Sulcata Maintaining the Good Health, Proper
Diet,
and Breeding of Tortoise

JOSEPH KINVEBOLG

TABLE OF CONTENTS

1 FUN AND INTERESTING FACTS ABOUT THE SULCATA TORTOISE........................1

2 WHAT MAKES A SULCATA TORTOISE A GOOD HOUSE PET? 4

    PROVEN TO HAVE A LONG LIFESPAN...4
    SAFE AND HARMLESS 4
    LOW-MAINTENANCE 4
    DOES NOT SHED..5
    EASY TO CLEAN AND GROOM..5
    LOVING AND FRIENDLY PETS..5
    MAKES AN ADORABLE PET 6

3 PURCHASING GUIDELINES: HOW MUCH DOES A SULCATA TORTOISE COST?....7

    PURCHASING GUIDELINES AND TIPS TO KEEP IN MIND 8
    BUYING THE SULCATA TORTOISE FROM A REPUTABLE BREEDER 9

4 PREPARING FOR THE ARRIVAL OF YOUR SULCATA TORTOISE: HOW TO
CREATE THE PERFECT ENVIRONMENT FOR HIM? 10

    GETTING THE RIGHT ENCLOSURE..11
    INDOOR AND OUTDOOR ENCLOSURE/HOUSING REQUIREMENTS 11
    LIGHTING AND HEATING REQUIREMENTS..12
    REQUIRED HUMIDITY...14
    RECOMMENDED SUBSTRATE..15
    FURNISHING REQUIRED IN YOUR TORTOISE ENCLOSURE..................................15

5 FEEDING YOUR SULCATA TORTOISE 17

    SULCATA TORTOISE AND THE RECOMMENDED DIET 17
    GRASSES AND HAY 18
    GREENS AND VEGETABLES..19
    FRUITS 20
    FLOWERS..20
    FRESH DRINKING WATER..21
    SUPPLEMENTS 21
    FOODS THAT ARE UNSAFE AND TOXIC FOR SULCATA TORTOISE......................21
    WHEN SHOULD YOU FEED YOUR SULCATA AND HOW MUCH?.........................23
    DO'S AND DON'TS IN FEEDING YOUR SULCATA TORTOISE 24

6 BEHAVIOR AND TEMPERAMENT OF SULCATA TORTOISES 26

    BEHAVIORAL PATTERNS AND TEMPERAMENT..26
    HOW TO HANDLE THE AGGRESSION OF YOUR SULCATA TORTOISE? 27

7 HOW TO INTERACT WITH YOUR SULCATA TORTOISE? 32

    HOW DOES THE SULCATA SHOW AFFECTION?..32
    COMMON EMOTIONS FELT BY THE SULCATA TORTOISE.......................................33

8 THE BASICS OF BREEDING...38

IDENTIFYING THE GENDER OF THE SULCATA 38
THE USUAL BREEDING SEASON 40
THE ACTUAL BREEDING PROCEDURES 41
HOW TO DETERMINE IF YOUR FEMALE SULCATA IS PREGNANT? 42
NESTING CONDITIONS IN CAPTIVITY 43
INCUBATION METHODS 44
THE HATCHING PROCESS 45

9 HOW TO KEEP YOUR SULCATA HEALTHY? **47**

EYES 47
CARAPACE (UPPER SHELL) 48
PLASTRON (BOTTOM SHELL) 49
SKIN 49
TAIL 50
NOSE AND MOUTH 50
MUSCLE TONE 50
OTHER FACTORS THAT DETERMINE A SULCATA'S HEALTH CONDITION 50
HEALTH ISSUES THAT YOUR SULCATA MAY ENCOUNTER 53

BONUS CHAPTER SUPPLIES AND ESSENTIALS TO INVEST IN FOR FIRST-TIME SULCATA TORTOISE OWNERS **55**

FOOD AND TREATS 55
INDOOR ENCLOSURE 56
HEAT LAMP OR INCANDESCENT LIGHT BULB 56
UVB LIGHT 56
HEATING EQUIPMENT 56
SHALLOW DISH 57

CONCLUSION **58**

1

FUN AND INTERESTING FACTS ABOUT THE SULCATA TORTOISE

Sulcata tortoise is a large reptile, which is also famous for its other name, African spurred tortoise. It is the third-largest tortoise species worldwide. It is a native tortoise of Africa, specifically the country's Sahel region located on the southern part of the Sahara Desert. You can also easily find the Sulcata tortoise in the savannah grasslands and deserts of Ethiopia, Senegal, and Niger.

One notable fact about this tortoise is that it can grow to more than 230 pounds and around 18 to 30 inches. This reptile is also capable of living up to 70 years. The friendly personality of Sulcata tortoise makes them amazing pets. This tortoise is even one of the best companions for pet lovers. Keep in mind, though, that this pet also requires the most proper care and maintenance to survive.

If you are interested in making a Sulcata tortoise your pet, then you have to try getting to know more about this species first. That way, you will know if it is indeed right for you to bring home one and take care of it.

Here are some of the fun and interesting facts about the Sulcata Tortoise that you should be aware of before deciding to live with one at home:

• **The skin of a Sulcata tortoise is quite thick** – It is often sand-colored or golden brown. On the other hand, the upper part of his shell, referred to as the carapace has a brownish shade.

• **Sulcata tortoise comes with an oval and broad carapace** – This carapace (shell) also has large scales referred to as scutes with each one having its own growth rings as coverings. The number of growth rings found in every scute normally depends on the tortoise's actual age.

• **The Sulcata tortoise thrives on a plant-based diet** – This specie is, therefore, a plant-eater or an herbivore. They often thrive on a diet plan composed of various grasses and succulent plants.

• **The sulcate tortoise's activity is based on the season** – In most cases, he is active during the wet or rainy season. The reason is that this is the time when he can easily access water and food. This tortoise also enjoys basking in the sun early in the morning as a means of increasing the temperature of his body. It is necessary in lifting his energy to ensure that he will have some for his regular everyday activities.

• **The Sulcata tortoise is naturally aggressive** – They are gentle pets but they are also naturally aggressive. You will even notice their ramming behaviors from birth. Expect this aggressive nature to become even more evident when the mating season comes.

• **During the hot season, the Sulcata tortoise stays dormant** – They also tend to be in the state of dormancy, also referred to as aestivation, during the hottest part of each day. In such a case, you will notice this tortoise digging burrows up to thirty inches in depth. They may also create complex tunnels up to 10-ft. in depth.

• **They belong to the crepuscular animals** – This means that they are more active during dusk and dawn.

• **They incubate for around 90 to 120 days (3 to 4 months)** – At birth, you can expect the hatchlings to be as long as 2 to 3 inches.

• **The Sulcata tortoise has rapid growth** – Expect one to double his length and size every three years. This tortoise also becomes sexually mature upon reaching 15 years.

• **They have strong survival skills in the wild** – They can even live for around 50 to 150 years if left to thrive in the wild.

These are just a few of the fun and interesting facts about the Sulcata tortoise that you have to be aware of. Note that while they are popular for pet lovers, they are also among the most demanding house pets, requiring a lot of your attention.

With that said, you should try learning as much as you can about the Sulcata tortoise before you finally commit to taking care of one. The good news is that once you decide to give it a go, you will be in for a treat.

Yes, they are demanding pets but taking care of one is truly rewarding and exciting. You will know exactly what makes them great pets in the next chapter of this book.

2
WHAT MAKES A SULCATA TORTOISE A GOOD HOUSE PET?

So what are the most rewarding benefits that you can get from taking care of a Sulcata tortoise? What makes them excellent house pets? Get to know the answers in this chapter.

Proven to have a long lifespan

One of the most striking qualities of a Sulcata tortoise is its ability to live a long time. In other words, you will have a friend who will be your companion for several years. You can enjoy being with this friendly pet for a long time, unlike other pets with shorter lifespans.

Safe and harmless

Another thing that makes a Sulcata tortoise an incredible house pet is that they are more harmless compared to dogs and cats. Yes, they also have the tendency to bite your finger whenever you put it inside their mouth but expect it to only cause minor damage. This makes them among the safest house pets, especially if you have kids in your household.

Low-maintenance

This is particularly true, especially during the winter season. Yes, you need to give them specific care and attention but once you have created the most suitable living environment and space for them, you can finally get rid of all your worries.

You can even expect your Sulcata tortoise to live with just a single healthy meal composed of leaves and fruits daily. Their diet plans are suitable for those on a budget. As for their home, you just have to make sure that there are external cooling systems as well as heat lamps around. These supplies can be of help in regulating the body temperature of these reptiles.

You will further notice how low-maintenance they are during the winter as they will naturally hibernate. The only thing that they need during that time would be a safe den so they can peacefully and comfortably hibernate.

Does not shed

The fact that Sulcata tortoise, and all tortoise species, for that matter, do not shed is a big advantage especially for those who have allergies. If you have a cat or dog allergy, then you are probably aware that a reaction may occur if you get exposed to their fur's dander.

These pets tend to shed over the items in your home, particularly your furniture. When they shed, they will also most likely leave particles in the air, triggering allergic reactions. If you do not want to trigger your allergy, then you may want to go for a pet who does not shed – one of which is the Sulcata tortoise.

Since they are hairless, you don't have to worry about your allergies. Moreover, they are great to look at, easy to care for, and highly affectionate, making them even more interesting as pets.

Easy to clean and groom

Compared to cats and dogs, a Sulcata tortoise does not require as much cleaning. The reason is that they are naturally clean. You have to bathe them regularly as it is what they need to stay hydrated but the whole process is not similar to when bathing a dog.

Apart from that, a Sulcata tortoise does not carry a foul smell. There are times when they will have a bit of a musty smell but it just happens occasionally. The majority of them are odorless, so you have an assurance that it does not require you to exert a lot of effort when it comes to grooming.

You can also free yourself from doing other grooming routines, like nail trimming, cleaning teeth, checking and removing ticks, and brushing fur. This can promote extreme convenience for you and your pet tortoise.

Loving and friendly pets

Contrary to what others believe, Sulcata tortoise makes an adorable pet considering their loving and friendly nature. A lot of potential pet owners mistakenly believe that all reptiles are emotionless creatures, making them think twice about making any tortoise species as pets.

It is time to get rid of that misconception, though. The reason is that Sulcata tortoise can actually give you the kind of companionship and love that you are longing for. Just like dogs who love playing as well as express their love, a Sulcata tortoise can also show that to his owners. They are also capable of showing affection as well as their likes and dislikes. It is even possible for your

Sulcata tortoise to seek your company most of the time, allowing the two of you to form a bond and connection.

In addition, the Sulcata tortoise is one of those pets who love to be stroked. You can please your tortoise through stroking in a couple of ways – one is stroking the skin surrounding his neck. It is a kind of petting, which directly shows your affection to him. Another way to do it is to stroke his shell. Yes, his shell is kind of hard, making you think that there is no sensation in this area, but that is wrong. Keep in mind that the shell of a tortoise comes with nerve-endings, making them feel the stroking and feeling pleased about it.

The fact that the Sulcata tortoise loves being stroked is a big help in strengthening your bond. It can make both your experience pleasant while letting you bring out the loving nature and friendliness of this pet.

Makes an adorable pet

Not yet convinced about the adorable nature of a reptile, such as the Sulcata tortoise? Then try looking for online videos of them eating strawberries or any other food being fed to them. Observe their tiny faces while munching down on fruit and you will surely feel pleased with the heartwarming scene right in front of you.

As you can see, owning a Sulcata tortoise makes you enjoy a lot of positive benefits. There are many good things about this reptile that make them truly great house pets. Just make sure that before you get a Sulcata tortoise as a pet, you research everything related to owning and taking care of one.

Ask yourself if you are committed to taking care of him, too. Note that while this pet is generally low-maintenance and tends to hibernate in some parts of the year, you still need to give him the care he needs when necessary.

Ensure that you are buying a tortoise from a legitimate and reliable source, too. You wouldn't want to get yourself involved in an illegal pet trade involving smuggled eggs or animals, would you? So be careful.

The next chapter will provide some important information regarding the purchase of a Sulcata tortoise. It will guide you throughout the purchasing and acquisition process, so you wouldn't end up transacting illegally.

3

PURCHASING GUIDELINES: HOW MUCH DOES A SULCATA TORTOISE COST?

If you have decided to get a Sulcata tortoise as your pet, then one of the key things you have to research is the cost of buying one. As the ideal pet tortoise, the Sulcata is perhaps the most taken cared of and kept one.

If you get the hatchlings, then you will most likely spend around $50 to $70. Because of their size, adult ones can cost higher. It can range from $600 to around $1,500 to $2,000. Adult tortoise is also costlier compared to the hatchlings considering the fact that the former already received a lot of care and investment from the owner.

The cost of a Sulcata tortoise also seems to differ depending on where you bought it. Some of the legitimate sellers of this pet are breeders, retailers, and tortoise keepers. Note that tortoise lives a long life, so expect to find a few keepers for just one Sulcata. Some also highly recommend buying one from a private seller as doing so will usually let you acquire other things, like the tortoise kits.

Purchasing Guidelines and Tips to Keep in Mind

When planning to buy a Sulcata tortoise, you have to be one hundred percent sure that you are getting it from a legitimate and reliable source. Avoid buying one from garden centers, pet shops, or over the web as much as possible. The reason is that it may put you at risk of buying a tortoise who is prone to developing an illness, eventually racking up the amount you will be paying for a veterinarian.

Also, remember that most tortoise species, like the Sulcata, slowly show signs of disease. With that, you may have a difficult time judging the state of health of a specific tortoise based on your initial observations.

Despite that, it is still advisable to do a complete physical exam. That way, you have a guarantee that what you will be getting is genuinely healthy. As a general rule, make it a point to check the ears, mouth, eyes, and noise of the Sulcata, so you will know if there is a discharge.

Spend time examining the shell, too. Find out if there is any sign of deformity or irregularity. In addition, the tortoise needs to be active, alert, and bright – all of which indicate that he is in his best shape.

It would also be in your best interest if you spend time examining your chosen tortoise and look for these signs that indicate how healthy he is:

• **Black pair of eyes that are clear, bright, and open**

• **Dry nose** – It should not show any sign of wheezing nor bubbling. The tortoise should not also breathe through his mouth. He should be able to do so using his nose.

• **Healthy pink tongue** – Observe the tortoise's mouth, too. Wait for it to open so you can assess the tongue. You will know that he is healthy if his tongue is pink and does not have any indication of bubbling. Moreover, the Sulcata needs to have a beak, which snugly fits. The uppermost beak should just cover the lower one.

• **Firm shell** – If you are getting a tortoise who is at least one month old, then his shell should be firm, not spongy nor soft. A tortoise who is in his first year of life, however, may still have a bit of spring to his plastron and that is acceptable. Despite that, the area where the plastron is should not be pink. Moreover, the shell needs to show no signs of damage nor cracks.

• **No hard lumps nor wounds** – The tortoise needs to be healthy enough that he does not have any hard lumps nor wounds on various parts of his body, especially the neck, head, legs, and ear area.

• **Clean tail area** – Another sign that you have to look for if you want to get a healthy Sulcata tortoise is a clean tail. Spend time examining the tail area and find out if it is naturally clean. The feces that passed through the Sulcata should not be runny nor loose. Moreover, worms should be non-existent in the feces.

• **Highly active in warm areas** – You also have to check how active the Sulcata tortoise is. You know that he is healthy if he seems to be genuinely and naturally active when he is staying in a warm area or environment.

Apart from the signs of good health that you have to find in a Sulcata tortoise before buying, you also have to check the legitimacy of the seller. You have an assurance that the seller is legitimate if he can provide the right documentation for the tortoise.

Also, in case the tortoise you intend to buy is microchipped, it would be highly recommended to seek the help of a veterinarian who should scan the animal. This scanning is essential in ensuring that all the microchip details provided by the seller perfectly match the tortoise.

Buying the Sulcata Tortoise from a Reputable Breeder

It would also be in your best interest to buy the Sulcata tortoise from a breeder who already earned an excellent reputation in this industry. As much as possible, pick a breeder who can provide you all the information you need about the animal's health history.

Remember that you will be with him for an extremely long time. With that said, you need to ensure that you begin your journey of having the tortoise as your pet on a healthy foot. You can achieve such a goal by ensuring that the breeder you have chosen is truly reputable.

The good news is that reliable and legitimate breeders are now easy to find in the US. The reason behind this is that the reptile continues to gain popularity. As mentioned earlier, you need to spend time doing a physical exam, which involves checking his physical attributes, especially the clarity of his eyes. If possible, make a request to witness the Sulcata when he is still eating. Note that a healthy one eats voraciously. If you notice that the one you intend to buy does not eat that way, or feeds himself too little, then it may indicate an illness.

The most important thing you have to do is to assess yourself. Your goal is to find out whether you are one hundred percent committed to adopting a large reptile that also has the tendency of outliving you. That said, ensure that you also set a plan regarding who you should assign to take care of him just in case he outlives you.

4

PREPARING FOR THE ARRIVAL OF YOUR SULCATA TORTOISE: HOW TO CREATE THE PERFECT ENVIRONMENT FOR HIM?

As indicated a while ago, the Sulcata tortoise is now a famous pet that is easily recognizable due to its huge size, large scales, and tan and brown shell. Before the actual adoption of this tortoise, try talking to the pet shops in your locality. You may want to re-home a senior already since there is now a huge number of Sulcatas in the world.

Once you have finally chosen the tortoise you intend to adopt or buy, make sure that you do all the necessary preparations for his arrival. It makes a great pet for a first-time reptile owner, like you, but you have to create the right environment for him – one that perfectly suits his personality and behavior, among many other things.

One key fact to take note of is that the Sulcata tortoise is usually a solitary pet. He often thrives when held captive provided you raise him in areas with hot and dry climates all year round. If you are living in such areas, probably in southern states such as Texas, then bringing home a Sulcata may be a viable move for you.

The fact that the Sulcata tortoise is huge is reason enough that you should house it outdoors. Also, keep in mind that this type of tortoise belongs to avid diggers. They have burrowing behaviors that may result in excessive damage to your yard if you are unprepared. Remind yourself of that fact before you finally set your tortoise loose in your backyard.

Getting the Right Enclosure

Of course, the first step that you have to take when preparing for his arrival and creating the most suitable environment for him is to get the right enclosure.

A constant reminder – this tortoise is not the average Greek-sized one who is capable of staying at a small and manageable size.

The shell of this tortoise can even grow up to around two to three feet (24 to 36 inches). Their weight will also go from 80 to more than 100 pounds. That said, you need to find a really huge enclosure for your new pet. It should not just be small nor medium-sized. You have to look for a big enclosure.

Here is a rough guide in choosing the right size of enclosure for your Sulcata tortoise:
• Small-sized Sulcata (around 2 to 5 inches in length) requires around 3 feet by 3 feet enclosure
• Medium-sized Sulcata (around 5 to 12 inches in length) requires around 5 feet by 5 feet enclosure
• Large-sized Sulcata (larger than one foot or one foot and a half) – If you want to take home the really large variety of Sulcata, then prepare to provide an enclosure that is large enough, making it close to the same size of a standard living room. If your Sulcata reaches this size, then you can move him to an outdoor enclosure so he can dig and move freely. Just ensure that the weather and climate meet the usual requirements for housing the Sulcata outdoors.

Indoor and Outdoor Enclosure/Housing Requirements

When preparing your home for the arrival of your Sulcata tortoise, remember that the best environment for them is that which allows them to have easy access outdoors for most parts of or the entire year. If you want to prepare an indoor enclosure, then it should have some flat and large rocks. These rocks are necessary as they file down the nails of the tortoise while providing them with a clean surface where they can eat.

You can also keep an outdoor enclosure if you are living in an area with warm weather. In such a case, ensure that you set the walls of the enclosure for at least 8 to 12 inches below the ground. It is necessary in preventing your Sulcata from escaping using the holes he may dig. Moreover, you need to set the enclosure walls 12 inches or higher above the ground.

Avoid using see-through walls and fences, too. The reason is that this may encourage the tortoise to escape over or through the walls. Use solid barriers and walls that will not let them see what is outside.

Also, keep in mind that Sulcatas are strong so you have to build the walls securely. You can further improve the stability of the wall with the help of cinderblocks. Moreover, this tortoise is an avid climber so put some rocks, logs, or other features that will help them scale. You may also want to integrate hiding places into their dens.

Another vital requirement for the indoor or outdoor housing would be shallow and wide dishes or pool where the Sulcata can soak. The highly recommended ones are mud wallows as these are the favorite spots of Sulcatas when it comes to soaking. One thing to note, though, is that this tortoise usually defecates when soaking. That said, the dish should also be small enough that the tortoise will not be able to soak in to drink.

If you housed over one Sulcata outdoors and you discovered some signs of them beginning to burrow or dig, then ensure to mark a flag on the specific spot where one of them has already dug or burrowed.

It will prevent you from losing track of the specific spot already burrowed by a Sulcata, thereby ensuring that you will not deal with a situation wherein more than one Sulcata consistently dig or burrow on the same spot. Note that this situation is dangerous as it may cause the tortoise to struggle to dig out.

Lighting and Heating Requirements

Sulcata tortoises can also be categorized as ectotherms. This means that they control the temperature of their body using the environment they are in. With that said, you need to invest in these three types of light for their housing especially if they are still indoors:

- **UVB light** – This type of light is crucial for the health and growth of your Sulcata. If you don't provide UVB light for your tortoise, then he will be prone to suffering from metabolic bone disease. The UVB light is also what your Sulcata needs to process calcium. Aside from that, it is necessary for Vitamin D3 production.

If you are still housing your Sulcata indoors, then make sure that his indoor enclosure has a source of UVB light. In this case, you may want to invest in light bulbs capable of producing UVB rays. If the Sulcata is already housed outdoors, then you can rest assured that he can readily get his much-needed UVB directly from the sun.

- **Heat lamp** – Also called basking spotlight, this is an essential supply for your Sulcata as it is what will provide the right amount of heat on even just one side of his enclosure. This heat will give him the warmth he needs, allowing him to bask in it when necessary.

- **Normal light** – You also need this light to make his enclosure bright enough, allowing him to see everything inside. Note that in most cases, if the Sulcata tortoise owner only uses a heat lamp, only a single part or side of the enclosure lights up.
  You may want to add a normal light inside to have an additional source of light and brightness. With that, the tortoise can see everything clearly. It is also a big help in training the Sulcata to distinguish daytime from nighttime.

If you plan to house your Sulcata outdoors, then it would be unnecessary for you to invest in the mentioned lights. The reason is that the area will be directly exposed to the sun that provides all the lighting required by the tortoise for survival. However, ensure that the enclosure makes it possible for him to burrow or dig underground as this will let him retain himself.

It is necessary for him to burrow sometimes, especially if he gets exhausted due to the extreme outdoor heat. By burrowing underground, the tortoise will be able to cool down no matter how hot it is outside. If you can't provide your Sulcata with an environment where he can burrow naturally or with the aid of a plastic pool bin or large pen in his enclosure, then it is advisable to just house him indoors.

Despite the need to cool down sometimes, the Sulcata tortoise also seems to thrive when he is staying in an environment with a hot temperature. The heat naturally helps him stay active and healthy. As a matter of fact, the Sulcata is capable of handling at least 100 degrees Fahrenheit for his outdoor temperature.

However, you still have to provide him with quick and easy access to a spot with enough shade so he can cool off whenever needed. At night, when the temperature goes lower than 50 degrees Fahrenheit, you should be able to provide a sort of supplemental heat.

You can use a basking lamp capable of providing up to 95 degrees Fahrenheit, so you can retain the recommended daytime temperature, which is around 80 to 90 degrees F inside the room, shed, or greenhouse where the tortoise lives. During nighttime, remember that temperatures that are around 60 to 80 degrees are usually fine.

Make sure that the enclosure does not get excessively cold, though, as it may ruin the appetite of the tortoise. This may cause him to stop eating and make him more prone to suffering from different kinds of illnesses.
If you plan to house the Sulcata indoors with temperatures that often go lower than 60 degrees Fahrenheit, then consider investing in a ceramic heat emitter. Use it in giving the tortoise sufficient warmth, allowing him to sleep in comfort even with the cold.

Required Humidity

The place where you put your Sulcata should have a humidity level of around 40 to 55 percent. Note that extremely high humidity might result in fungal infections, among many other possible issues. With that said, you need to make sure that the required humidity is always met within the tortoise's enclosure.

You can reach the required level of humidity by picking the right substrate. Alternatively, you can mist the enclosure two times a day, preferably once every morning and evening. If it does not work, then mist it more frequently. You may also find a digital hygrometer (otherwise called humidity gauge) useful as it can help you measure the actual level or percentage of humidity easily.

If you notice that the humidity in your Sulcata's enclosure is not enough, then some things that you can do to increase it and meet the requirement are:
• Use a thick layer of your chosen substrate – This should make it possible for the substrate to increase the thermal energy and liquid it can hold.
• Spill water into your chosen substrate.
Introduce well-misted and adequately watered live plants in your Sulcata's enclosure.
• Use a humidifier to mist his habitat frequently.
• Add a water dish, or any other similar item, to the enclosure.

- Trap humidity in the specific areas where the tortoise often hides.
- By doing any of the mentioned tips, you can increase the level of humidity a bit, preventing you from worrying too much about it not being sufficient.

Recommended Substrate

As mentioned earlier, you can use a substrate in order to reach the required humidity within your Sulcata tortoise's enclosure. A substrate is necessary because it allows the tortoise to burrow and dig in. Aside from that, the most appropriate substrate is necessary in increasing the level of humidity in case it is lacking.

The most suitable choice for a substrate would be a mix of play sand and topsoil. Make sure that the two are in equal amounts when mixed. You may also use equal amounts of play sand and coir and combine them to create the substrate.

You can also find other substrates in case you can't get a hold of the mentioned mixture. Among the substrates you can use in this case would be the aspen mulch, orchid bark, and cypress mulch. Change the substrate every week to make the most out of it. You also need to scrub the enclosure using warm water and soap once every month.

In case you intend to house the tortoise outdoors, ensure that the area has a lot of non-toxic grass. This should give him enough material for grazing. There should also be sufficient soil where he can bury himself. Moreover, you need to keep the pen clean by removing the food scraps and excrements in there every day.

Furnishing Required in your Tortoise Enclosure

To ensure that the housing or enclosure of your tortoise can make his stay in your home so comfortable, you also need to furnish it with the right materials. Among the furnishing you have to invest in and gather to make your Sulcata tortoise survive are:

- **Large water dish** – This item is where you can see the tortoise soaking in and drinking water from. Go for a water dish, which has enough depth to ensure that a substantial part of his shell will get wet. However, it should not also be too deep that your tortoise will be at risk of drowning.
Position this water dish in a cool spot of your enclosure. The reason is that the integrated heat lamp may cause the dish to dry out quicker than expected. It

may also cause the water to warm up. This is not good for your tortoise as it may prevent him from freshening up using cool water.

• **Hide box** – It would also be helpful to invest in a hide box. Put it in the cool part of your pet's enclosure. The good thing about this hide box is that the tortoise can use it in retreating whenever he feels scared or threatened. The box is also useful in case he is looking for a spot to sleep in.

Go for a hide box proven to be sturdy. If you are building a really huge enclosure for your pet, then a dog house may also be used as a hide. Just put it inside, so your tortoise can hide in it anytime.

• **Various toys enjoyed by the tortoise** – Research the wide range of toys that the Sulcata tortoise may enjoy. Among these items would be rocks and tunnels. Your tortoise will also most likely feel happy if you put logs inside his enclosure. He will use these items to stay active, allowing him to climb over, through, and under.

While some furnishings are essential for the enclosure, make sure not to overdo them. This means you should stop yourself from overdecorating the enclosure. This will prevent it from getting extremely filled up, still leaving enough room for the tortoise to move around freely. Once you have everything prepared, you can finally welcome your chosen Sulcata tortoise into your home.

5
FEEDING YOUR SULCATA TORTOISE

One distinctive quality of a Sulcata tortoise is its voracious appetite. With that said, you need to supply him with the right diet to keep him in tip-top shape. Caring for this tortoise and making him your house pet also requires understanding the best foods to feed him. It is the key to making him enjoy the best quality of life possible.

When it comes to feeding your Sulcata, one thing you should instill in mind is that this pet is an herbivore. In other words, he primarily feeds on plants. Grasses are even the main sources of food for Sulcatas in the wild. Similar to sheep and cows, you can classify the Sulcata as a strict vegetarian and herbivore.

With that, expect this tortoise species to graze fibrous and dry grasses and hays. Most of them also tend to ingest blossoms and fruits occasionally. If you intend to bring one home as a pet, then be prepared to create a diet plan for him consisting of dark and leafy greens, like mustard, collards, red leaf lettuce, and Romaine lettuce. Your Sulcata tortoise will also most likely thrive when sticking to a diet plan composed of foods rich in fiber and calcium while being low in protein and fat.

Sulcata Tortoise and the Recommended Diet

For a Sulcata tortoise to survive as a house pet, you have to feed him with the right foods. Note that most of those who own one refer to the tortoise as an eating machine. The reason is that this tortoise tends to forage and graze for several hours during the day. Sulcata also tends to eat a lot.

If held captive, you should be able to give this tortoise species an environment that lets him graze on weeds and grasses devoid of any herbicides and pesticides, among many other chemicals. Another thing you have to know about Sulcatas is that they tend to evolve when living in a semi-arid environment, which means that dry grasses and weeds are the only foods available for them the entire year.

What they need specifically is a grass-based diet rich in fiber to keep their health in tip-top shape. Keep that in mind, so you can feed him the right foods. Note that feeding him incorrectly may cause him to grow too quickly. Your tortoise will also be at risk of developing a pyramided and bumpy shell as well as some health issues that may shorten his lifespan if you let him eat the wrong foods.

Basically, his diet plan should consist of the following:

Grasses and Hay

Once you have decided to take care of a Sulcata tortoise, you should create an environment for him that allows him to access hay and grasses easily for grazing anytime. This easy access to hay and grasses is also essential considering the fact that those make a huge part of their diet (at least 90 percent specifically).

With that said, you need to make sure that the grasses you are going to feed him grow within his enclosure, allowing him to graze anytime he wants throughout the day. If possible, make the grassy area within his enclosure around 6 feet square as this would be enough to meet his daily razing requirements.

If you can grow grasses for him, then you don't have to worry too much. You can still offer grass cuttings, such as Bermuda grass, and mix it up with around 50 percent of leafy greens guaranteed to be safe for tortoise, like turnip greens, mustard greens, grape leaves, collards, watercress, dandelion greens, and endive. To guarantee the safety of these foods for him, make sure that they are free of herbicides or pesticides.

During the summer, you can just grab your scissors and cut the grasses from your yard and put them in a bucket, so you can feed your Sulcata with them. Note that the majority of grasses growing in yards are safe for Sulcatas to eat. Just make sure that they are untreated with chemicals.

During the winter, the time when most grasses stop growth, feed your Sulcata with Timothy or orchard hay as they are great replacements for the grasses. Other types of hay that you can safely offer to your Sulcata are oat hay, orchard grass, and meadow grass.

A lot of pet stores and department stores sell these hays, so you will have no problem finding them. If you want to save, then the cheapest solution would be to visit a farm supply store and buy in bulk. Another way to get your hands on the hay that your Sulcata can eat is online. You can just order online and wait for it to get delivered to your doorstep.

Greens and Vegetables

Your Sulcata tortoise's diet should also consist of some greens and vegetables. In fact, fresh veggies should compose around 10 to 15 percent of his diet. Some of the greens that are good for Sulcata are the following:

- Dandelion greens
- Turnip
- Kale
- Collard greens
- Mustard

When it comes to feeding him with greens, remember that you should limit the ones rich in oxalate. Some of them are spinach, rhubarb, beet greens, and parsley. They are generally safe for your pet but it would be best to give only moderate amounts of them. Also, make sure that the greens and veggies you offer your Sulcata are appropriate for him. The reason is that some veggies are unsafe for Sulcata tortoise as those may cause them to suffer from long-term health issues, like impaired thyroid function and gout. To guide you, here are the safest vegetables that are good for him:

- **Snow peas**
- **String beans**
- **Acorn squash**
- **Barley**
- **Bell pepper**
- **Turnip**
- **Butternut squash**
- **Sweet potatoes**
- **Lentils**

- **Carrots**
- **Bok-choy**
- **Pumpkin**
- **Romaine lettuce**
- **Kale**
- **Corn on the cob**
- **Winter squash**

To feed him with veggies, make it a point to chop them first. They should be in bite-sized pieces. Serve the veggies by putting them in a bowl or shallow plate first. This will prevent the tortoise from consuming sand together with the veggies.

Fruits

You can also feed your Sulcata with fruits, though, it would be best to do it sparingly. You should give fruits to him only as occasional treats. The reason is that fruits are rich in water and sugar, and Sulcatas are not that used to receiving both while they are still in the wild.

While this tortoise is fond of the sweetness provided by fruits, their digestive systems are made in such a way that they can't digest excessive amounts of fruits that well. Among the fruits that are safe enough for your tortoise are cantaloupes with rind, peaches without pits, berries, apples, pears, apricots without pits, strawberries, and chunked organic bananas that still have their skin on.

Just constantly remind yourself that this species is not used to sugary foods, so do it occasionally to avoid harm. Also, remember that the key to giving him proper nutrition and letting him enjoy every treat you offer him is variety. With that said, moderation is key to ensuring that any food, including fruits, will not harm his health.

Flowers

You can also feed some flowers to your Sulcata tortoise. Just make sure that you choose those that are not toxic to him. Some of your options if you are looking for non-toxic and safe flowers to feed your Sulcata are roses, nasturtium, hibiscus, and dandelions. It would be best to stick to the mentioned blossoms and double-check first whether the other flowers you intend to feed him are safe and non-toxic.

Fresh Drinking Water

Your Sulcata tortoise also needs fresh drinking water every day in order to survive. It is important to note that this tortoise does not actually consume excessive amounts of water since he gets most of the water, he needs from the foods he eats. However, you still have to supply him with water religiously since there is a guarantee that he will drink enough if he sees it in front of him.

With that in mind, ensure that there is a wide and shallow bowl for his water when he is still young. Clean it every day since there is a possibility that he will defecate in the water. He will also most likely use the water for soaking, which is good for his health especially when done twice or thrice a week.

If you are living in a place with high temperatures, then do not use a metal-based bowl where he can soak as it is possible for him to suffer burns from it. It would be best to go for a ceramic bowl, which you can purchase from a pet store. It is easy to clean and affordable while also being constructed in a way that the specific and unique needs of the tortoise are greatly considered.

Supplements

The Sulcata tortoise is in need of high levels of calcium as a means of strengthening his shell and keeping himself healthy. Most of his daily recommended intake of calcium can be derived from dark leafy greens. However, it also helps if you incorporate a powdered calcium supplement into his diet. Just make sure to seek the help of a vet before making him take in a supplement, though.

Pick a supplement made specifically for reptiles. Also, ensure that you read the instructions particularly the dosage. The reason is that you have to stick to the recommended dosage to guarantee the safety of your Sulcata.

To use the required supplements, you can sprinkle some powder on leafy greens. Put an antler, cuttlefish, or pieces of bones in the enclosure so he will have something to chew. You may also want to add a powdered vitamin supplement made for reptiles to the leafy greens you intend to feed him. That way, you have an assurance that your pet will receive all the nutrients he needs not only from foods but also from his supplements.

Foods that are Unsafe and Toxic for Sulcata Tortoise

One thing to note about the Sulcata tortoise is that even with his tough outer bits, he is actually usually sensitive inside. This house pet does not also have a natural ability to determine if something is bad and unsafe for him.

With that said, you have to take extreme caution before feeding him something. That way, you will have peace of mind knowing that he will not nibble on tortoise foods that are harmful and extremely toxic for him.

One risk when it comes to feeding the Sulcata is their tendency to eat toxic plants in the garden. It is the reason why you have to know exactly what is in your garden or yard before you allow him to roam. Make sure that anything that may cause potential harm to your tortoise is gated. It is also advisable to prune them and ensure that they are out of reach of your tortoise.

In that case, here are some foods that your Sulcata should not eat:
- **Nightshade**
- **Belladonna**
- **Morning glory**
- **Citrus leaves**
- **Ivy**
- **Wild mushrooms**
- **Sage**
- **Rosemary**
- **Chinaberry fruit**
- **Cucumber**
- **Mushrooms**
- **Celery**
- **Cabbage**

Some foods also lack nutritional value for a Sulcata, so it would be best to avoid them as well. These include bean sprouts, zucchini, cauliflower, broccoli, radishes, and lettuce. You can feed him parsley, kale, and spinach but do so only occasionally. The reason is that such foods might lead to organ and bone issues if he takes them regularly and excessively.

Cooked or processed foods that humans consume should not also be fed to your Sulcata. The reason is that such foods are most likely too high in protein, water, and salt, making those unsafe for him. Avoid feeding him plants that are extremely high in protein, too. Some examples are beans, avocados, nuts, soy, and peanuts. Do not give him grains, cereals, and bread as well.

Aside from that, animal protein, such as meat, cheese, and eggs, is also prohibited. It is because this type of tortoise is incapable of handling high-protein foods, unlike other reptiles. Moreover, he should not include insects, fish, and mice in his diet.

One exception to all these prohibitions, though, is when the soil in his environment is extremely low in calcium. If that is the case, then your tortoise will most likely be unable to get a good supply of this vital nutrient. You can solve this issue by spreading his food with ground cuttlefish bone or eggshells but do it only once every week.

When Should You Feed Your Sulcata and How Much?

The process of feeding your Sulcata is quite simple. You just have to allow him to graze in the yard the entire day and provide him with the foods he is allowed to eat several times a week. Remember that this pet should be able to grow steadily and slowly. Too little or too much and it may lead to pyramiding.

In case he is still indoors, give him a pile of foods approved to be safe for his consumption daily. The pile should also be as big as he is. If he is still a baby, you can feed him around one-fourth cup of weeds, grasses, and greens daily. Do this until he reaches around six months. At around 6 to 12 months, your Sulcata can thrive with one-fourth to one-half cup of the recommended and approved foods daily. Young and juvenile Sulcata tortoises are capable of eating around one cup daily. In case you intend to feed him with pellets, then the goal is to provide him just around one to four percent of his body weight.

However, if you notice that he devours all the food you feed him even if he is still a baby, then it would be safe to increase the quantity a bit. You may also consider giving him a smaller snack or meal in the afternoon.

If he is already an adult, your goal should be to give him easy access to a yard containing safe grasses so he can eat anytime he wants during the day. Aside from that, it is highly recommended to feed him greens daily as a means of supplementing and adding variations to his diet. One head of radicchio or Romaine lettuce is often enough to make him both healthy and happy.

You should also remind yourself that you can't expect all Sulcata tortoises to develop similarly. This means it would be unnecessary for you to starve him but you should also avoid stuffing him with too many foods either. The bulk of his diet should always be grass. Eventually, you can determine the exact quantity of foods he has to eat to become full without getting engorged.

Do's and Don'ts in Feeding your Sulcata Tortoise

• **Make fresh water accessible for him every day** – The belief that this type of tortoise does not need water considering it is a desert species is a misconception. Your pet specifically needs water to avoid dehydration and other serious illnesses.

• **Ensure that your Sulcata receives enough fiber** – Feed him a fiber-rich diet by ensuring that his meals are predominantly based on grasses. It should also consist of a few edible weeds, flowers, and leaves.

• **Stay away from foods that may prevent the absorption of calcium** – Supply your Sulcata with just sufficient amounts of calcium. Note that this mineral is crucial for the healthy growth of his shells and bones, so he needs foods that ensure that his body receives adequate calcium.

• **Do not feed him with foods that are extremely high in protein** – With that said, you have to avoid including any kind of dog or cat food, dairy products, cheese, legumes, grain products and grains, as well as other tortoise diets known for being commercially available.
It is also best to ensure that you do not feed him with veggies in extremely large quantities. The reason is that all kinds of produce cultivated mainly for human intake, including dark leafy greens, have extremely high amounts of protein for Sulcata to thrive. With that in mind, you can give these foods to him, although just occasionally and in small amounts only.

• **Do not give him excessive amounts of fruit** – Yes, your Sulcata loves fruits but avoid giving these fruits to him excessively. Note that as a grazing tortoise species, the Sulcata greatly depends on the beneficial bacteria found in the intestines to digest as well as extract nutrition or nourishment from all that he eats, specifically grasses.

Giving him too many fruits may also cause the sugar and acid content to change his digestive tract's pH level. Such a change may result in the damage of the beneficial bacteria found in his gut. You can prevent that from happening by limiting his intake of fruits. You can still give him some, especially if he loves fruits, but keep in mind how important moderation is.

• **Do not overfeed him** – Keep in mind that this tortoise runs a risk of suffering from various health issues if you feed him the wrong foods. Your Sulcata may also experience some problems, even if he is eating the right foods if you feed him huge amounts all the time. This is what we call overfeeding and is a huge mistake often committed by a lot of tortoise keepers.

Remember that reptiles usually have slower metabolisms compared to mammals, such as cats and dogs. With that in mind, there are instances when he would become incapable of taking in too many foods.

Aside from the mentioned do's and don'ts, it is also advisable to consider his current activity level. Is he a pet who can roam around your secure yard or go outdoors daily? Or is he one of those who remain indoors and stay in a tiny table specifically made for him? If you notice that your Sulcata has a sedentary lifestyle, then it would be unnecessary for you to feed him daily. Your pet can actually survive with feeding every other day. Just make sure to stick to what foods are recommended for him.

6
BEHAVIOR AND TEMPERAMENT OF SULCATA TORTOISES

One incredible fact about most Sulcata tortoises is that they are famous for having great personalities, provided their owners keep and care for them properly. They are capable of living for several decades, making it possible for them and their owners to develop a strong bond.

If you plan to take one home, then it would be best to learn more about his behavior and temperament. That way, you will know exactly what to expect from him as far as his personality and behavioral patterns are concerned. Your knowledge about this tortoise's personality is also helpful in interacting, dealing with, and bonding with them more effectively.

Behavioral Patterns and Temperament
Basically, the Sulcata tortoise can show signs of shyness and friendliness. They may also show aggressiveness from time to time or a mix of all the mentioned behaviors. In most cases, female Sulcatas tend to display a shy personality.

Males, on the other hand, are often the friendlier ones. They also seem to display the behavioral patterns of dogs. However, this observation does not necessarily mean that all male tortoises are not shy and all females are not outgoing. You can still find some of them that seem to have switched personalities.

The fact that this tortoise is bigger in size compared to other pets is also a reason why he moves slow. Moreover, some of them display curiosity. A healthy Sulcata tortoise may be curious about a lot of things.

There are even times when such curiosity is detrimental to them. It may cause them to get trapped in small places, particularly those that are not suitable for their size. The curious behavior of a Sulcata may also be the reason for him to flip over without being capable of correcting his stance or position.

Sulcata tortoises are also famous for their burrowing or digging tendencies. This is something you should be aware of if you want to take proper care of this popular house pet. One tends to burrow or dig the ground to form holes that are up to ten feet in depth. You should keep that in mind since if he makes a hole close to a building or home, then it is greatly possible for it to damage or destroy the foundation.

Generally, this tortoise is docile and pleasant when taken care of as a house pet. However, there are rare cases when he gets territorial and aggressive. Watch out for signs of his territorial or aggressive personality as if you do not handle it properly, then there is a tendency for damage to take place. These behaviors combined with their burrowing tendencies may be destructive. For instance, he may damage or ram properties or hurt the people around him. He may ram at anyone surrounding him, including animals and people, whenever he feels the need to defend his territory. It is mainly because he is territorial over his space.

Another thing about his behavior that you have to be aware of is his constant need and want for food. You may notice this behavior in your own Sulcata, too. However, you have to avoid misconstruing his tendency to beg for food constantly as a sign that he wants attention. Note that he displays such behavior just because he truly wants food.

While some behavioral patterns of Sulcata are quite bad, you will be glad to know that they also have several positive traits. This means that they still make fantastic house pets despite some of their bad traits. You just have to tame your tortoise a bit or create the perfect environment for him, so he will constantly display the most favorable behaviors.

How to Handle the Aggression of your Sulcata Tortoise?

Just like what has been mentioned a while ago, the Sulcata is an approachable and friendly reptile, making one a fantastic house pet. However, there are also instances when he becomes too aggressive, moody, and territorial.

You do not have to worry too much, though, since with proper care and attention, your Sulcata can curb his aggression or lessen his tendencies. You also have to investigate a bit about his temperament, so you can immediately spot his aggression and deal with it appropriately. It also helps in reducing his aggression significantly.

One thing that you can do to handle your Sulcata tortoise's aggression as soon as it comes is to know its triggers. That way, you can create an environment for him that is devoid of the common triggers of his aggressive nature. Among the most common triggers for such behaviors are:

• **When the female tortoise carries eggs** – If you are taking care of a female tortoise, then note that one part of her life is carrying eggs. The problem with egg-carrying female tortoises is that there are specific instances when they feel threatened, prompting the need for them to keep their eggs protected.
If she feels that way, then she may display some forms of aggression. You can see some females holding an aggressive stance with their necks being extended and their legs set on high. Other aggressive behaviors that these females may show are hissing, biting, and bobbing heads.

• **Keeping two male Sulcata tortoises inside a similar closure** – It is possible for a male Sulcata to display aggression if you keep him inside an enclosure together with another tortoise. If that happens, then the two may get territorial, causing them to fight or display their aggressive behavior towards each other. This is their way of showing and proving their dominance. There is also a possibility for the two of them to become aggressive if they want to mate with just one female.

• **Hunger** – Another possible reason why a Sulcata suddenly gets aggressive is hunger. If he is hungry, then he may also suddenly transform into an angry pet. He will most likely turn into a fussy eater. If that happens, then he may only eat those he likes, instead of those that provide his body with nutrition. Furthermore, he may also become aggressive if the foods he can access are not enough or if the food selection is not to his liking.

• **Lack of stimulation within his enclosure** – The lack of stimulation may cause your Sulcata to get bored, frustrated, and aggressive. With that said, make it a point to put anything inside his enclosure that will keep him preoccupied. It could be toys and balls, anything that will occupy his mind and get rid of stress.

• **The constant intrusion of people** – This trigger can be characterized by people constantly coming inside his enclosure. Just think of it from your own perspective. You would not want people to keep coming inside your private space, right? Still, this "intrusion" will depend on the mood of your Sulcata, as well as how good his enclosure is and his relationship to the one who gets inside his private space.

Your knowledge and understanding of the common triggers of the Sulcata's aggression can help you avoid an episode. This means that you should not worry too much about his aggressive nature since there are scenarios that you can avoid to make him feel safer and more comfortable, thereby significantly lowering his aggression.

Now the question is, how will you find out right away that your Sulcata tortoise is starting to become aggressive? Are there evident signs? Keep in mind that this famous house pet often communicates his feelings through various postures and stances. When it comes to dominance and aggression, expect him to communicate it with a posture composed of an elevated body and head.

Also, remember that he may misconstrue the manner through which you handle the situation as threatening or aggressive. A shy Sulcata tortoise, for example, may feel threatened if you turn him upside down. With that said, you have to be extra careful when it comes to dealing with it.

You will also know if your tortoise starts to become aggressive if he shows the following signs:

• **Banging of the head** – This often signifies that a reptile, like the Sulcata tortoise, begins to become assertive. He may bang or knock his head on anything, even the specific object that causes his aggression. The Sulcata may also bang his head to mark his territory and assert his dominance.

• **Snapping or biting** – Your tortoise may also snap or bite every time he gets into a fight with another reptile. Note that the powerful beaks of this tortoise are enough to cause pain to the one he has bitten. There are even captive situations wherein the aggressive tortoises bite handlers. In most cases, the trigger is the feeling of threat and frustration. Sticking your fingers inadvertently into his mouth may even lead to him biting you.

• **Chasing** – There are times when the tortoise will chase his handler aggressively. It could be during that time when he feels territorial. However, remember that chasing can't always be pointed to aggression. There could also be other reasons for it. For instance, if he is hungry, then it is greatly possible for him to chase or run after you once he sees you because he is excited to devour the food you may have brought to him.

Some Sulcata tortoises also urinate and ram to display their aggression. Just make sure that all these signs can be pointed to aggression before you deal with the behavior specifically. Make sure that you do not misinterpret the signs. Also, avoid handling this behavior excessively, especially when the tortoise is still young and fragile.

If you handle the situation excessively, he may get stressed out, causing some health issues, including those that may cause his premature death. With that said, handle his aggressive nature correctly and ensure that the handling is not too extreme.

The following simple tips can also help you deal with his aggressive nature:

• **Do not put two male Sulcatas inside one enclosure** – However, if you intend to take care of two males, then it would be ideal to introduce the two of them to their enclosure simultaneously. This means both of them should be around when you give them a tour of their enclosure. By doing that, there is a low risk for one of them to feel like he has to protect the private space he owns for a longer time.

• **Provide plenty of space for roaming and burrowing** – The enclosure should have adequate space so your Sulcata will not have a difficult time roaming around and burrowing. It is crucial to put enough substrate inside the enclosure, too. This is important as inadequate space in a small enclosure may only make your tortoise feel too aggressive.

• **Offer enough food and water** – Make sure that your tortoise can choose from a wide range of foods. There should also be enough water within easy access. This is especially important if the enclosure contains more than just one tortoise. By doing that, they will not feel like they need to compete for food and water.

• **Avoid overhandling your tortoise** – This means you should not pick him up nor turn him upside down or over whenever he becomes aggressive. The reason is that this may only make your tortoise even more uncomfortable. There are even those who do not want being handled, particularly those who are not well-socialized yet.

• **Do not spend too much time inside his enclosure** – Instead of spending time with him in his enclosure, allow him to go out and move in an area that both you and he can share. By doing that, he will never feel like you are imposing on his territory. This tip is even more important especially once your pet becomes an adult.

Generally, your tortoise does not want to be picked up just like what has been indicated earlier. However, it does not necessarily mean that he does not like and appreciate human contact. You can still hand-feed and pet him to strengthen your bond without stressing him out.

Also, being large in size may cause discomfort for both you and him whenever you decide to carry him. With that said, try to just let him be himself with his four feet on the ground and bond with him that way. This is the key to bringing out his positive qualities, like being outgoing and friendly, and trumping the negative ones, like his aggressiveness and dominance.

7

HOW TO INTERACT WITH YOUR SULCATA TORTOISE?

Now that you are aware of the good and bad behaviors that your Sulcata may display, you are probably wondering how you can make sure that you are interacting and connecting with him correctly. As his owner, you are eagerly waiting to strengthen your bond. But the question is, do Sulcata tortoises act the same as the other usual pets, like a puppy or cat who love to snuggle with their owners?

Are these pets capable of getting attached to their owners? Do they show affection similar to a pet bird or any other mammal? The answer is yes. All it takes is to learn how to interact and connect with him correctly. It could be different from the way other mammals and pets show affection, though. Still, Sulcatas often display their love and affection to their owners through scent, sound, and body language.

How Does the Sulcata Show Affection?

Identifying when and how your Sulcata starts to show affection is crucial in figuring out how you can effectively communicate and interact with him. One thing you have to remember is that he is not like other common pets who may run up to you and beg you to cuddle or pet him. This tortoise species will most likely sit in just one spot, feeling contented seeing his owner around.

The Sulcata loves watching humans every time they feel affectionate to him. He may also show signs that he is specifically interested in the thing you are doing while he is close to you. In some cases, he stretches and lengthens his neck while you are around to show that he wants you to rub or scratch him.

You will also sense right away that he wants affection once he closes his eyes and leans in to feel your touch.

You can't see your tortoise jumping up and down when he sees you, though. Despite that, you can still rest assured that he feels a bit excited about you entering his room, especially if you have brought some tasty treats. The way he displays his excitement is just different from other pets, though. In most cases, he will walk slowly towards you. He may also pace the enclosure slowly so he can grab your attention.

Another thing that most Sulcata tortoises do to show their affection is positioning their nose close to you, so you can touch it with your arm or hand. It is a common social trait while this species is still in the wild. He may also follow you around or bump against you. If you notice that, then it is possible for him to want you to pat him a bit.

It would be best for you to stimulate and encourage this affectionate behavior so he will be able to develop it even further. You can do so by talking to him and showing him that you love to visit him every now and then.

Common Emotions Felt by the Sulcata Tortoise

Learning how to interact with your Sulcata tortoise effectively is also all about understanding the most common emotions he may display. Note that just like humans, your tortoise also feels different emotions. Some of the most common ones that you have to be aware of if you want to interact and communicate with him correctly are:

• **Curiosity** – You will know right away that your tortoise feels curious about something if he constantly pokes and looks around his enclosure. It could be because he is trying to find a delicious treat to nibble in. He may also be curious about how to get some steps in.

• **Boredom** – This emotion in tortoise is one of those you have to try to control and avoid as much as possible. The reason is that if your Sulcata tortoise gets bored, then his destructive behaviors will most likely become imminent. Among the destructive acts he may display out of boredom are overturning food bowls and water dishes, climbing out of his cage desperately, and digging up plants. Prevent that from happening by filling his enclosure with toys or anything that will entertain him. You may also want to schedule play sessions with him outside his enclosure.

• **Jealousy** – Another powerful emotion that your Sulcata may feel is jealousy. Note that the jealousy shown by this reptile is unlike the ones felt by humans. However, this feeling in Sulcata may lead to him displaying a couple of unwanted behaviors.

It mostly happens if you put more than one male tortoise in the enclosure. The reason is that this species does not often get along with other males. There is an even higher likelihood for this to happen if you have a female tortoise inside the enclosure since males will most likely fight whenever the mating season arrives. In most cases, though, this jealousy is a result of wanting to have manly dominance inside their environment.

• **Friendship** – Your Sulcata may also display the emotion of wanting to be friends with you or another tortoise. However, even if you feel like he shows signs of wanting to have friends, you have to conduct research before adding new mates in his cage or enclosure. You have to analyze his behavior first and find out if it is really what he wants.

If you figured out that putting more than just one Sulcata in the enclosure is the best thing that you can do, then ensure that you have the resources to increase the space they can roam around. If possible, triple the space where you intend to keep them in. Keep in mind that most tortoises are naturally territorial, so having more than enough space for them is essential.

• **Fear** – Yes, your tortoise will also feel scared or afraid of something. One sign of fear is when he pulls his limbs and head back to his shell. There are even cases when the tortoise tries to run. It is crucial to detect fear as soon as possible so you can put him at ease and prevent trauma. You also have to identify the source of his fear so you can at least remove it from his sight and enclosure.

• **Pain** – The fact that the Sulcata tortoise has a huge shell is one reason why there are those who wonder whether this reptile is capable of feeling pain. If you are one of these people, then take note that the answer is yes. This means that they feel pain both emotionally and physically. In some cases, you will notice this tortoise wincing whenever he gets hurt. You will also obviously notice if he feels grief and sadness.

• **Happiness** – A Sulcata tortoise who receives proper care, love, and attention will also feel happy and content. One sign of his happiness is when he sits in one spot with his head and limbs relaxed. You will see these parts coming out of the shell. It shows that he is in a relaxed stance. You will also know that he is happy and content if he seems to look for his favorite human.

Basically, your goal is to interact with your tortoise the right way, so you can make him feel happy and content above all the other emotions he can feel. When he is happy, you will love seeing him chill out, dig, and be out in the open. He will also most likely swim, munch on things, and become more social. It would be best for you to focus on bringing out this positive emotion, so both of you will have a wonderful time together.

Communicating and Interacting with your Sulcata

Now that you are aware of the emotions that he can display and how he displays affection, it is time to learn some tips about how you can effectively communicate and interact with your pet Sulcata. One thing that you will surely love about the Sulcata is that they can recognize their owners and caretakers. It may take time, though, but you can rest assured that they are smart enough to recognize their owners soon enough.

Once you have one as a pet, you can train him to recognize your sound, scent, and unique traits. That way, he will be able to associate your presence with food, love, affection, and safety. Basically, the successful interaction between you and your tortoise will all boil down to him recognizing you as his owner or caretaker and you understanding his unique traits and how you can make him happy.

Since it will be unlikely for your tortoise to learn how to speak the language of humans, it would be best for you to bridge your communication gap. You can do so with these tips:

• **Handle your shy Sulcata gently** – If your Sulcata tortoise displays signs of having a shy personality, then ensure that you handle him gently. It is actually advisable to do so even if your Sulcata is not the shy type, but it is crucial to follow this tip even more if he indeed has that trait.

Note that tapping his shell, picking him up all of a sudden and unexpectedly, and flipping him over without warning can be viewed by him as acts of aggression. This species often experiences such treatments from a rival while in the wild. With that said, avoid doing such acts and treat him kindly and gently instead.

• **Move slowly when dealing with him** – Note that quick movements may stress your tortoise. Such may indicate aggression to him. He may view quick and sudden movements as his rival coming to him, prepared to trample over him or flip him over. To make sure that you will not stress him out, avoid being in a rush when approaching him. Move slowly, so he will calm down.

• **Give him gentle and soft touches when needed** – You will know right away if he wants to be touched so make sure to give in. It would be best to touch his legs, head, and shell gently since doing so will show gentleness and curiosity. Never touch his nose without any warning since it is one of the most sensitive parts of his body. If you touch it carelessly, then you will be at risk of hurting him.

• **Breathe steadily whenever you interact with him** – Keep in mind that the Sulcata takes heed of a person's breathing pattern. As a matter of fact, he views it as a natural and normal part of interacting or communicating with others. It is the reason why you have to breathe steadily whenever you come to him.

Avoid heavy and laborious breathing when you are close to him since he may view it as a hiss, a sound of submission or fear for him. Heavy breathing combined with your heaving body may even cause him to misinterpret it and look at it as a challenging posture. With that, he may act defensive and aggressive.

• **Practice bobbing your head** – Do it when you are with your tortoise. Note that bobbing is not only a part of a mating ritual. You will also notice him bobbing his head slowly when he feels calm and relaxed. You can mimic this act to show that you are also relaxed and you want to establish a friendly rapport with him.

If he looks at your face, bob your head. In case you notice that he likes to see things on his level, then use your thumb or fist to imitate the act of bobbing the head. Believe me, your Sulcata will look more adorable once he bobs back.

Most tortoises, including the Sulcata, are often solitary animals. It is natural for them to seek privacy, but in captivity, you can still expect them to recognize their owners. They can even show fondness and affection. Your tortoise may even see you as someone who can keep him safe and give him pleasure through foods and treats.

Be prepared to spend time creating the bond, though. Keep in mind that with the long lifespan of Sulcata, it is natural for them not to rush things and be more purposeful. You can rest assured, though, that with time, you can finally create that bond. Just do your research before bringing one home, so you will know exactly how you can effectively interact and communicate with him and turn him into your perfect companion.

8

THE BASICS OF BREEDING

Breeding is also one of the things you would like to know if you are planning to take care of a Sulcata. This holds true, especially if you have a wonderful experience caring for one and you have plans of increasing the number of tortoises you take care of at home. The good thing about the Sulcata species is that it has a higher chance of being bred anywhere. As a matter of fact, it is one of the most produced tortoises worldwide.

Several decades ago, you can rarely see this species in the US. Recently, though, the Sulcata tortoise showed its ability to adapt to different habitats and climates while being in captivity. The low cost associated with caring for them and breeding them together with their amazing personality (despite their aggressive and dominant behaviors sometimes) is the reason why most first-time tortoise owners seek this species.

Identifying the Gender of the Sulcata

When it comes to breeding, one thing you should do is to learn how to identify a Sulcata tortoise's gender. It can be quite difficult since all Sulcata tortoises when they are still babies or at a young age look like females. In fact, it takes quite some time (years even) for you to identify your Sulcata's gender accurately.

To find out whether he is a male or a female, he needs to reach around 12 inches in length and weigh approximately 15 pounds. Once it is already the right time for you to identify the gender, there are several factors and parts of the tortoise that you can use to guarantee accuracy. These include the following:

• **Plastron** – The plastron refers to one of the main parts of a tortoise's shell. It is specifically the shell's bottom underbelly. You can use this to identify the gender at the right time since male and female Sulcatas have different shapes for their plastron. In most cases, you can identify a Sulcata as a male if he has a concave plastron. A female Sulcata, on the other hand, often holds a flat plastron.

• **Anal Scutes** – You can find these vital parts of the Sulcata on the plastron, particularly at around your pet's tail. You can easily find the two scutes as they are shaped like a "V". By checking out the anal scutes, you can detect the gender of your Sulcata. Males often have anal scutes that come with a wide flare. Meanwhile, female ones have narrower anal scutes.

• **Gular Scutes** – You can see these parts at your Sulcata's plastron by the head. One sign that you have a male sulcate if his gular scutes are long and large. The fact that they have longer and larger gular scutes than females make them use these parts to dominate the other males. In most cases, male Sulcatas even use these gulars to flip or ram other tortoises.

• **The flash** – Of course, this is the most common sign that your Sulcata is a male. He will most likely flash you using his private parts.

• **Mounting tendencies** – If you have a male Sulcata, then he will most likely love mounting other tortoises. Note, however, that mounting does not always mean that you have a male tortoise who intends to breed. It may also signify his desire to show and display his dominance towards another.

Mounting may also indicate a male wanting to mate a female tortoise and trying to dominate other males. You can't be one hundred percent sure that you have a male Sulcata based on its mounting tendencies alone, though. The reason is that there are also females who tend to mount others. Still, the likelihood that you have a male is high because they are the ones who display such behavior more often.

• **Aggressiveness** – You can also detect whether a Sulcata is male or a female based on the level of aggressiveness. Note that while both genders are prone to showing their aggressive nature every now and then, you can see males showing it more traditionally. This is especially true when they are with other males.

With the aid of these factors, you can figure out whether your Sulcata is a male or a female, promoting ease once you decide to breed.

The Usual Breeding Season

Once you are already aware of how to identify the gender of your Sulcata tortoise, your next concern will most likely be how to start breeding. One thing that you have to know about this tortoise species is that they are capable of producing plenty of eggs annually. In other words, it is necessary for you to look for suitable and appropriate homes for a max of one hundred baby Sulcatas every year if you are serious about breeding them.

Also, you should know that this tortoise is capable of breeding once they hit the early age of five and upon reaching around 25 to 40 pounds. Male Sulcatas also tend to mature sexually before the female ones. To guarantee the health of your female tortoise, it is advisable to wait until she is old enough for breeding. In most cases, she needs to be at least ten to fifteen years old to be able to handle breeding without hampering her health.

In terms of the breeding season, it usually begins when January starts and lasts until December. Basically, it happens for a year. On average, though, males begin mating around the month of February or at the end of a rainy season. You can't expect to detect a set breeding season for this animal, though. The reason is that they are capable of breeding the entire day.

Also, you will notice that male Sulcatas will try mating a female whenever he sees one or every now and then. It varies depending on the mood of the male. During the time the Sulcata tortoise breeds, the female is often subjected to stress. The reason is that males tend to be confrontational whenever they want to breed. As a matter of fact, they are willing to fight others not only for dominance but also to show their admiration for the female Sulcatas.

The females often start looking for areas where they can nest around two months after they mate. Note that they are often very selective when it comes to finding nesting sites. In fact, it often takes up to two weeks for them to find the right spot. It takes around one to four hours for a female to finish her nesting site. After that, she will start laying an egg every few minutes.

In most cases, the female Sulcata lays eggs every five to six weeks often during the months of January to May. You can expect her to stop laying eggs once it gets too warm or hot. As for the gestation period, it often takes around sixty days after mating. The females are capable of laying a max of six clutches containing ten to twenty eggs at once. This means that you will be able to get around fifty to a hundred eggs annually. In this case, you have to invest in one or two incubators to ensure that the eggs will hatch.

The Actual Breeding Procedures

In the wild, the Sulcata tortoise can be expected to have a stronger urge to mate during the spring season and after hibernation. This mating urge also depends on the geographical location of the tortoise. In a few Mediterranean coastline locations, it is possible to find tortoise mating frequently at chance intervals the entire year.

In the wild, the mating process starts from courtship. Basically, the male will pick up the scent trail of the female, going after the trail until he gets his ultimate target. This is when the courtship starts. It will then be followed by mating, gestation, and the nesting and laying of the eggs.

The same process also happens when you take a Sulcata as your house pet and when he is in captivity. However, since the tortoises are not in their natural environments, you have to make an extra effort to make the breeding and mating processes work. The first thing that you should do is to look for suitable partners.

As much as possible, only breed the same species (in this case, the male and female Sulcatas only). Note that it is only rare for incompatible mating to result in fertile eggs. If it happens, then it is also possible for it to have numerous health risks. The fact that the mating is incompatible may cause the eggs developed in the females to get malformed. They may be misshapen or get too large that it will be hard to express them safely. It may also cause signs of distress for females during the laying and nesting periods.

With that in mind, it is essential to make sure that you only mate Sulcata species. Avoid looking for another species with the hopes of forming a hybrid. Another vital requirement when it comes to finding suitable partners is to choose only the younger ones. The younger ones are, of course, more suitable for breeding, since they are considered to be more fertile. Do not subject older Sulcata females to the stress and strenuous efforts associated with mating and laying of eggs. It is because this might compromise their health.

Once you have perfectly matched a pair of Sulcata tortoise (same species, perfectly healthy and young, free from past eggs, and similar sub-species), you can finally put them inside an enclosure together. Once you have introduced them, expect the male tortoise to display his aggressive nature to start the courtship right away. It may happen for a prolonged period while the tortoises are in captivity, especially if there is not enough room that allows the female tortoise to escape.

There are instances when the actual mating or copulation process gets short-lived. However, it is also highly likely for it to happen repeatedly. As much as possible, stick to letting the Sulcatas have only brief mating encounters. You can make that possible by putting the suitable partners inside the enclosure for only two hours or so per day. Also, do it only for a few days. This period should be enough to produce a successfully fertilized egg.

The brief mating encounter is also advisable to lower the risk of injuries caused by butting or biting. If you notice open wounds in any part of the tortoise body, then make sure to treat them right away. Separate them immediately, too. Once the mating ends, you should give the female tortoise easy access to more calcium. That way, she will have a higher chance of forming healthy eggs. It is also necessary for the health and well-being of future hatchling. Continue to give her easy access to calcium until she has completely laid all eggs.

How to Determine if your Female Sulcata is Pregnant?

After the mating of your male and female tortoises, you will probably wonder how you can detect right away if it results in a successful pregnancy. Note that after mating, the female is capable of storing the healthy sperm of the male for a max of three years. However, this fact does not mean that you have access to viable eggs for three years, but it is highly likely.

If the female Sulcata gets pregnant, keep in mind that you will not see a visible and noticeable baby bump. However, you can detect her pregnancy if she starts to display behaviors that are not normal to her, including:

• **Increased crankiness and agitation**

• **Aggressiveness towards female Sulcata tortoises and humans**

• **Sudden desire to protect her private space** – If she shows that sign, then it would be best to separate her from the others.

• **Digging more intensely compared to before** – You may also notice her looking for and testing nesting spots in her habitat.

• **The tendency to use her nose as a means of nudging the ground** – She does this to test the level of moisture and the softness of soil.
• **A sudden slowing in her eating pace**

If she shows the mentioned signs, then she may already be pregnant. You may also do the following steps to detect whether she has eggs.

Step 1 – Lift your female tortoise. Do it gently to ensure that you do not agitate her and cause her to become aggressive.
Step 2 – Move the back of her legs and ensure that they do not get in the way.
Step 3 - You should then insert one of your fingers within her abdomen. Do so using gentle pressure. She may not be pregnant if the area feels squishy and soft to your touch. However, if that part is quite firm, then it is greatly possible that she is pregnant and what you felt is an egg.

You should avoid doing this activity too often, though. The reason is that this may stress out your tortoise. As someone who is interested in breeding Sulcatas, you should also be observant to the female ones, especially during their pregnancy. Observe for some signs that indicate they have problems, like breathing difficulties, swelling of the head, swollen and red eyes, loss of appetite, edema, and runny nose.

Certain issues on a pregnant female's shell, sudden weight loss, and spots on her skin could also indicate a problem. If your female Sulcata shows the mentioned signs of pregnancy problems, make it a point to contact a veterinarian right away. That way, you can act right away in case her pregnancy is something to be concerned about.

Nesting Conditions in Captivity
Since the tortoises are in captivity, you need to make sure that you create artificial nesting areas for them that are close to the natural nesting conditions they are used to in the wild. One way to do this is to prepare a large cold frame or ordinary garden greenhouse for them. Make sure to fence off glass panels that your tortoise may directly come in contact with to avoid accidents.
Create a huge load of earth, too. It should consist of 60 percent topsoil and 40 percent sand combined together at the center of the greenhouse. Heap the mixture to create a mount that is at least 18 inches deep. You also have to invest in an incandescent basking lamp. Hang it exactly above the mount. It should be at a distance that allows you to achieve a 30-degree Celsius soil temperature

steadily.

Leave the greenhouse like that for around twelve hours every day. The pregnant or gravid female should be able to access this greenhouse easily and whenever she wants. This technique can encourage her to lay eggs in just a few weeks.

Incubation Methods

As for the incubation, note that there are several methods that you can implement to make it happen. Among these methods are floating the eggs in containers or tropical fish tanks and keeping the eggs in airing cupboards. The most reliable method of incubation nowadays involves the use of an adapted bird-egg incubator or a specialist reptile incubator you can buy from a shop. Take note, though, that the success of the incubation depends on a couple of factors. It is possible to succeed depending on your ability to keep the egg in a specific environment that adheres to the following criteria for success:

• **Proper temperature** – You can expect the eggs of the Sulcata tortoise to incubate successfully only if the environment they are in has the correct temperature. In most cases, the temperature should be in the range of 25 to 35 degrees Celsius. If you let them incubate in an area with a temperature lower than 25 degrees Celsius, then there is a high risk for the hatchlings to not develop.

If the temperature is too high, though, over 35 degrees Celsius to be exact, then it is highly likely for the development to become too quick. This may lead to losing moisture content too fast, which can eventually cause the death of the hatchlings. Make sure that the incubators you have maintain the correct temperature to guarantee success.

• **Correct humidity** – It is also important to maintain the right humidity needed for the whole incubation period. In that case, the humidity level you have to maintain needs to be around 50 to 90 percent. A humidity level that falls below the required minimum may cause the contents of the egg to dry out.

Going beyond the maximum humidity level, on the other hand, may cause the eggs to drown due to excessive water absorption. If you want to have an easier time measuring humidity so you can correct it right away, then you can invest in humidity digital probes. Some even come with temperature digital probes. You just have to put this item inside the incubator to read both humidity and temperature accurately.

• **Egg disturbance** – It is crucial to keep the eggs of your Sulcata tortoise in a similar way until the first days of incubation come. Note that if an egg gets disturbed (ex. it gets turned upside down), then it is possible for the yolk sac to smother the hatchling that it is trying to develop. With that in mind, ensure that you pick an egg incubator that can already easily adapt to the surroundings to prevent the contents from getting disturbed.

Also, keep in mind that during the development period, the hatchlings are prone to experiencing stress easily. It is the reason why you have to minimize handing. It would be best not to disturb the eggs to avoid unnecessary risks. The less disturbed the eggs are, the higher their chance of developing and eventually transforming into hatchlings.

As for the actual period of incubation, note that it starts from the moment you put the eggs inside your chosen incubator up to the time they hatch. This period varies depending on the incubation temperature and humidity, among many other relevant factors. Generally, it lasts for around 50 to 150 days. A higher temperature in the incubator can speed up the hatching process. However, this does not mean you should force to increase the temperature beyond what is recommended just to get it to hatch quickly. It may only cause malformation or death.

The Hatching Process

While still in the eggs, you can expect the baby Sulcata tortoise to be folded in half literally. The fold could be across their plastron. They also appear almost round. They get the chance to straighten out once they absorb the majority of the yolk sac that support their life. When this happens, you will notice their small carapaces being pressed directly to the egg shell, leaving an imprint of the texture of the shell. You can clearly see such an imprint starting from hatchlings until they grow.

Soon enough, you can expect the hatchling to straighten out until it reaches such a degree wherein it can puncture a tiny hole in the egg shell using its bony protrusion. This protrusion, which is also otherwise referred to as an egg tooth can be seen being developed at the end of the snout.

The egg tooth forms holes that cause the shells to dry out and weaken, breaking them open while the small tortoises emerge. If you want the entire process to be successful, then prevent yourself from interfering, especially during the time of hatching. You should only interfere if it clearly shows that the tortoise is seriously in trouble.

Note that some of the tortoises may escape within just a few minutes of puncturing the egg. Another thing you should remember is that even those tortoises that come from a similar clutch do not automatically mean that they will also hatch together. Moreover, it was discovered that it usually takes a max of three weeks from the first hatching to the last to come out safely.

Right after they come out of the egg, make sure that you provide them with a shallow bath using lukewarm water. This is important in removing the sticky membrane that may have surrounded them. It is also essential in ensuring that they get to have their first drink.

9
HOW TO KEEP YOUR SULCATA HEALTHY?

Once you get a hold of your Sulcata (whether it be from breeding or from buying one), you have to commit to giving him the best of health. If you intend to buy a Sulcata, then choose an active and alert one. He should have clear and bright eyes. It is also advisable to purchase this tortoise from a reliable and reputable source to ensure that it will be alive and healthy once it reaches you.

However, even if the Sulcata is at its optimum health once you lay your eyes and hands on him, it is still crucial to learn about the possible health issues that may plague him. That way, you can prepare and avoid them as much as possible.

You also have to check some parts of his body from time to time as doing so can help you detect how healthy he is. The following are a few of the parts of the Sulcata tortoise's body that you have to monitor constantly:

Eyes
While this tortoise does not have the same huge eyes that dogs and other pets have, you can still use his eyes to monitor how healthy he is. Check whether his eyes are alert, shiny, and bright as such indicate that he is at the pink of health. It should not be too dry as this may signify an illness or dehydration. However,

his eyes should not also be excessively wet, weepy, or runny as such may indicate an infection. This means you should never neglect any discharge that you notice on his eyes.

Also, remember that injuries trigger blindness. With that said, check his retinas every now and then to see if there are scratches. Make this a regular part of his maintenance routine. Avoid worrying too much, though, if you notice his third eyelids show from his eyes' front corners as such scenario is completely normal.

However, it is important to act on it if you notice that his eyelid is closed all the time. It could mean that his eyes are injured. It may also indicate that your tortoise is ill or dehydrated. Do not pry his eyelids open, though. Make sure to let a veterinarian or an experienced handler do it for you to guarantee your tortoise's safety.

Carapace (Upper Shell)

Observe his carapace or upper shell regularly, too. Being the most visible part of his body, it is, therefore, your best hope when it comes to examining his heath. It is also the specific part that you have to look into if you want to see if he is growing healthily. The reason is that the condition, size, and shape of his carapace or shell can say a lot about his health condition even if he is still a hatchling or a baby. You will have an even easier time assessing his health through the carapace once he ages.

One thing that you have to check is the firmness of the shell. It is because a firm shell combined with relative smoothness indicates excellent health. If you notice any cracks, dips, and lumps in his shell, then it is highly likely that he is injured or ill. If he got injured in the past, then the irregularities in his shell could indicate that there is something wrong with him internally.

Also, keep in mind that the shell also grows when your tortoise grows. In that case, he should be able to display growth rings, though these rings should not be quite similar to the ones in trees. You can count the growth rings that your tortoise has to have an estimate of his age. Remember that the growth rings that old tortoises have are usually worn-down or already faded, so you can't still have an accurate estimate using the rings for older ones. The condition of the growth rings is also affected by changes in climate as well as the differences in health, nutrition, and environment eventually.

Plastron (Bottom Shell)

You will also get an idea about the present state of health of your Sulcata using his plastron or bottom shell. This part is even identified as the tortoise's stomach. Similar to the upper shell, the bottom also needs to be firm or hard. When they are still hatchlings, you can expect them to have a bit softer plastron. However, it will most likely harden or firm up fast.

You will also know that the plastron is healthy if it is devoid of any sign of damage. It needs to be smooth while being perfectly sealed. A severely scarred plastron or one that is newly injured indicates the existence of internal damage. It is often caused by trauma, like being mistreated, experiencing dog bites, and falling on any hard surface, like a rock.

Skin

Spend time checking the skin of your Sulcata tortoise, too. A healthy tortoise skin is characterized by it being tough and rugged. It should cover his stocky limbs and should be tough enough to fend off even prickly barbs as well as deal with rough terrains. You will also know that he is healthy if his skin appears kind of dry and wrinkly.

If you notice his skin becoming moist or wet, then it is highly likely that there is a problem with his health. However, his skin should not also be too dry as it may also result in sores and cracks. Either way, you should never delay your visit to the veterinarian.

When you notice your tortoise shedding his skin, do not get alarmed right away. Never peel off the skin when that happens, too. The reason is that it will naturally come off. This means that pulling the skin off deliberately may only result in injuries that could hurt your tortoise and cause infection.

Another sign of good health that will be visible on the skin is the absence of any open wounds or sores. Keep in mind, though, that the older Sulcatas may have skin that shows a few visible scars. Do not assume that they are injured right away as it may only be a result of aging. However, it helps to note the locations where the scars appear. Observe the area every now and then to find out if they reappear.

Another thing that you should do is to check the skin for any parasites, like mites and ticks. The reason is that these parasites are at risk of digging close to your Sulcata's shell, the specific part where you can see the softest skin.

Tail

Often the most overlooked part of a tortoise when it comes to doing a health check, it is time to examine the tail of your pet every now and then. You have to ensure that your tortoise shows a clean tail as much as possible, which somewhat signifies good health.

In other words, it should be free from any dirt, like caked-on feces and urates. Spend time checking the tail for any cracks or sores, too. Moreover, find out if there is any sign of damage or irritation in the area. That way, you can detect right away if his health is at risk.

Nose and mouth

You also have to examine his nose and mouth regularly. One way to check whether he is healthy is if he has a clear and pink mouth. You will also notice that his beak is a bit longer on top while being curved slightly downward. It is also crucial for the beak to not stay open or crooked for a prolonged period.
As for the nose, make sure that it is clear. If he has a runny nose, then make sure to understand what causes it right away. Also, certain factors, liked caked debris, dirt, and sand around your tortoise's nostrils, are signs that he has a past illness. Aside from that, he should not have any bubbly discharge from either his nose or mouth as it indicates a severe illness. In that case, visit a good veterinarian right away.

Muscle tone

You may also want to spend time checking the muscle tone of your tortoise to find out if he is healthy. If he is weak or flaccid, then it is highly likely that he is dehydrated. It could also mean that he is dealing with a serious health issue, so be vigilant for any other signs.

You will know right away that your tortoise is healthy based on his muscle tone if he has strong muscles. Moreover, the tortoise needs to be able to stand tall. He should be capable of lifting his plastron from the ground, which is a sign of good health. If he seems to be a bit saggy or does not like to stand all the time, then he may be ill or experiencing stress.

Other Factors that Determine a Sulcata's Health Condition

Aside from his body parts, it also helps to assess the health of your Sulcata based on his displayed behavioral patterns. Note that while the personality of Sulcatas differ every now and then as some of them are shy while the others are dominant and outgoing, they still have common grounds. This means that there is something about their individual personality that will point out that they are happy and healthy.

For instance, you can expect a healthy Sulcata that feels at its best to be active. You will notice him actively moving and roaming around his enclosure. During playtime, your Sulcata will also most likely display his curiosity. You will notice his strong desire to explore.

You can also see him quickly moving to his points of interest. A tortoise whose personality is more on the strolling and curious type will most likely move purposefully. He will also do so with strong and even strides. In case he gets lethargic, he may feel sick. It is also possible that he is sick if he moves using slow, labored, and dragging steps and if he lets himself get tucked within his shell all the time.

You also have to check his appetite. Considering the large size of Sulcatas, they most likely belong to those known as ravenous eaters. Some of them will even continue to eat long even if they already had enough. It sometimes results in obesity. One way to find out whether your tortoise is healthy is to find out if he constantly has a good appetite.

In case he stops to eat all of a sudden or gets picky with food, then it is highly likely that he does not feel well. However, take note that there are instances when the lack of appetite can be attributed to overfeeding him with a lot of treats. With that in mind, you have to be extra cautious and ensure that you only feed him enough, especially in terms of treats.

In addition to his appetite and activity level, it also helps to check the following to determine if your tortoise is indeed healthy:

• **Poop** – It also sometimes helpful to check your tortoise's poop to find out if he still has good health. Note that the simple act of looking at his leavings can help you determine if he is stressed, sick, dehydrated, or healthy. If he passes poop regularly, then you may not have to worry about his health.

Also called feces, the poop can be identified as your tortoise's solid waste products after digestion. The normal color is often greenish-brown or brown. This shade will greatly depend on the foods he eats. For instance, if your tortoise eats plenty of leafy greens, then it is highly likely that his poop will appear green, too.

Make it a point to check the frequency and consistency of your tortoise's poop. If he feeds less frequently, though, then expect his poop to become less frequent. However, it still differs from one tortoise to another, so ensure that you are fully knowledgeable about your own pet's personality.

When the poop comes with a whitish layer on top of a dark base or if it is just generally white, then do not worry too much. It could only be because he defecates and urinates simultaneously, which happens frequently. The process may include him passing whitish urates, causing them to sit atop the poop.
Also, keep in mind that the look of a healthy poop in a tortoise sometimes varies widely. However, what it should be not is being dry, gritty, or hard. This means you need to consult a veterinarian right away just in case your tortoise starts to strain whenever he needs to pass feces, urates, and urine.

Moreover, take note of any immediate changes in your tortoise poop's consistency, smell, and frequency. You have to be more observant just in case these changes remain unexplainable even if you greatly consider his diet. For example, if the tortoise begins to defecate hard pellets all of a sudden and once every three days even if you have not changed his diet, then it may be a source of concern, prompting the need to contact a veterinarian.

• **Urine** – Urine refers to the liquid part of his leavings. In most cases, it appears as a splash of water. There are also instances when it looks like some puddle that has been left inside a tank. Some torts, however, urinate in the water used for bathing, which means you may have a difficult time seeing this liquid unless you observe closely.

The normal color of urine for a tortoise is white. It may appear like some spilled milk. If his urine is similar to that, then you do not have to worry because it may signify his good health. The problem is when the urine looks like red streaks or puddles forming around the tank.

There are also times when this urine comes in other unfamiliar and strange shades. If that is the case, then there is a great possibility that his kidneys or bladder are not that healthy.

• **Urates** – These refer to the results when the body of your tortoise starts to process protein. In most cases, these urates appear as creamy, pasty, and white substances. You can resemble them to toothpaste in terms of the way they look. You can expect these urates to be passed whenever you urinate. The reason is that just like your urine, it is also the bladder that stores the urates.

One thing to take note of, though, is that the urine and urates tend to come simultaneously. It is the reason why the two often combine, producing a milky white mess. It should look that way; otherwise, there could be some problems with your Sulcata's health. If the urates he passes are either dry or gritty, then such could indicate a health problem.

Make it a point to check all these factors and parts of his body regularly so you can immediately act on any imminent problem that could be affecting his overall health.

Health Issues that your Sulcata May Encounter

One thing that you have to take note of about the health problems often encountered by Sulcatas is that such often results from a poor diet as well as unwanted living conditions and environments. Among those that you have to watch out for include:

• **Calcium deficiency** – It may manifest in various ways – the most common of which are the softening of his shell and the development of metabolic bone disease. You can prevent that from happening by ensuring that his diet is safe and appropriate for him. Aside from that, you have to make natural sunlight, as well as a UVA/UVB light source, easily accessible for him.

• **Respiratory disease** – Most Sulcatas also suffer from respiratory ailments. In most cases, this can be characterized by nasal or eye discharges. Other signs of respiratory issues in Sulcatas would be raspy and noisy breathing patterns. You can prevent that from happening by ensuring that he sticks to a healthy diet.

• **High protein** – You will know that your Sulcata has an abnormally high level of protein that significantly hampers his health if he shows shell pyramiding as well as the buildup of uric acid in his bladder.

If those signs appear, then it is highly likely that he will face a life-threatening health obstruction affecting his urinary tract. Again, this problem is preventable. All it takes is to give him the healthiest and most appropriate diet.

In addition to the common health issues mentioned, he may also be at risk of suffering from the following:
• **Shell infections**
• **Dehydration, which often affects hatchlings and juveniles**

- **Nutritional disorders usually caused by metabolic bone disease**
- **Abscess**
- **Bladder stones**
- **Ticks**
- **Diarrhea**
- **Intestinal parasites**

Also, be wary of the behaviors displayed by your tortoise. For instance, if he gets excessively lethargic, displays some symptoms of illness, or has a poor appetite, then it would be best to contact a veterinarian right away so his condition will be evaluated. Make sure to choose a veterinarian who already has experience in handling and treating reptiles.

Do not let him suffer from an illness for a prolonged period of time. The reason is that it might lead to him suffering from irreversible kidney and liver damage. In that case, have him evaluated by your veterinarian right away. Among the tests that he has to undergo would be bloodwork and radiographs – the results of which are effective in assessing his present health condition more accurately while helping the veterinarian find the most suitable treatments.

Remember that your lack of knowledge about how to care for your tortoise properly may cause his health to be in danger. There are even cases when the tortoise in captivity dealt with premature death because of lack of information.

Do not delay visits to an experienced reptile veterinarian, so your tortoise will be able to undergo his routine health checks. It is also crucial in examining your tortoise for the presence of parasites, thereby preventing several serious diseases. It is also the key to giving you the support you need in your attempt to build a satisfying and long relationship with your Sulcata.

BONUS CHAPTER
SUPPLIES AND ESSENTIALS TO INVEST IN FOR FIRST-TIME SULCATA TORTOISE OWNERS

Now that we have already covered some of the most important aspects of owning and caring for a Sulcata, let's include in the final chapter of this book the common supplies and essentials that will help you complete your preparation for the arrival of your new house pet. Note that you can fully prepare for his arrival by ensuring that you invest in the right supplies and essentials – those that your chosen Sulcata will most likely need.

By having the following supplies and essentials, your Sulcata will surely turn into a happy and healthy pet even if it is still your first time to take care of one:

Food and Treats
Being strict herbivores, you need to invest mostly in vegetation, so you can feed your tortoise the right way. In that case, his diet should primarily consist of grass and weed. Moreover, your tortoise should stick to a low-nutrient and high-fiber diet to guarantee a slow yet stable growth.

Buy those foods that are sure to provide him with the nutrition he specifically needs. You may also want to invest in hay, which you can use to give him something to munch on and prevent hunger after you feed him with fresh grasses or any other food appropriate for him.

Prepare some treats for him, too. If possible, start a garden composed of the foods and treats he will most likely love. Add life to his diet by incorporating some treats into it, like coneflower, rose, mint, violets, geranium, grape leaves, dandelion, marigold, clarkia, Aloe Vera, and pumpkin.
Another thing to take note of is that calcium is a crucial part of his diet. Some great sources of calcium that you can safely feed to your Sulcata tortoise are mulberry leaves, grapes, and Dandelion greens. Make sure that his enclosure comes with a cuttlebone, too. That way, he can eat anytime he wants.

Indoor Enclosure

Of course, you will also most likely love to provide him with the most appropriate indoor enclosure. Create his enclosure in such a way that his health and happiness will not be compromised. You also have to invest in things that will surely make his enclosure look similar to his natural environment in the wild. You can even make housing for him using wooden tables, wooden bookshelves, and tubs.

Heat Lamp or Incandescent Light Bulb

You need this to put atop the tank. It is an essential supply as it is what will give your Sulcata a warm basking area. Ensure that the light bulb helps in making the temperature in the area reach around 95 to 100 degrees F when you turn it on. If it does not help in that regard, then it is advisable to adjust the bulb's wattage as you deem fit.

UVB Light

You also need to have a UVB light before you bring home the Sulcata tortoise you intend to take care of. This is a vital item as it aids in processing calcium while your tortoise is in captivity. The absence of this type of light can be harmful to your tortoise as it might cause him to develop severe health issues, such as metabolic bone disease and shell growth abnormalities.
If you are making your Sulcata stay in a pen with an open top, then make it a point to position the UV light across the top. There should also be a heat lamp that you securely clamp to one side. Alternatively, you can set the lamp on top in case a screen is present.

Heating Equipment

Another great investment that can guarantee the health and wellness of your

Sulcata tortoise is any heating equipment. Note that various types of heating equipment can be used by your tortoise. There is what we call the ceramic heater, which supplies plenty of heat. This heater also works in heating up a huge enclosure or space.

Another item that falls in the heating equipment category is the halogen bulb. It is a nice item to own as the use of it aids in the development of the shell of your tortoise. One more thing that you can invest in is the rheostat, which you will surely find useful in the effective control and regulation of lighting temperature within his enclosure.

Shallow Dish

This item is specifically important for babies. The reason is that it will hold the water that they need to stay hydrated. It allows baby Sulcatas to gain easy access to water anytime they want, thereby preventing health issues caused by lack of water intake, including kidney stones and kidney failure.

Make sure to pick a dish, which gives you a hundred percent assurance that the baby tortoise will not drown in case he flips over or fall while inside the dish. Once the tortoise reaches adulthood, you can provide him with a water bowl using a flower pot's bottom dish. Again, it should be designed in a way that your tortoise will have a zero risk of drowning.

CONCLUSION

Taking care of a Sulcata tortoise may be challenging at first, especially if it is still your first time to own one. However, with proper research and by ensuring that you gather as much information as you can about this reptile, you will surely be armed with all the things you need to make both your lives as endearing as possible.

Just remember how important it is to feed him the right diet and ensure that his environment meets all the requirements, particularly in terms of temperature, heat, and light. By doing that, you have an assurance that your tortoise will grow healthily and happily.

Do not hesitate to give him your full attention every now and then, too. It can help make your bond stronger and ensure that he will turn out to be the best companion for you. Hopefully, all the information that you have gathered from this book will help your life together with your new house pet becomes even more interesting.

Good luck in your journey towards taking care of one of the most adorable house pets on the planet, the Sulcata tortoise!

Made in the USA
Monee, IL
05 October 2022

15250816R00035